BARCELONA

THE CITY AT A GLANCE

Museu Marítim
One of Spain's finest
Gothic architecture.
Avinguda de les Dras...
www.museumaritimb...

CCCB
This striking cultural c...
the MACBA, Barcelona'...
museum, designed by Richard Meier.
See p042

Las Ramblas
Barcelona's most famous boulevard is a
tourist mecca, but charming all the same.
La Rambla

Park Güell
Gaudí's fantastical park is one of his most
playful creations.
Carrer d'Olot, T 93 219 3811

El Ajuntament (City Hall)
The focal point of the old city.
Plaça Sant Jaume, T 93 402 7000

Sagrada Família
Gaudí's unfinished masterpiece and
symbol of Barcelona.
See p045

Museu Picasso
See the artist's early work on display
in a row of medieval mansions.
Carrer Montcada 15-23, T 93 256 3000,
www.museupicasso.bcn.es

El Mercat del Born
Visit the fashion boutiques surrounding this
impressive wrought-iron structure, currently
being converted into a cultural centre.
Passeig del Born

INTRODUCTION

THE CHANGING FACE OF THE URBAN SCENE

In the 1990s, Barcelona set the standard by which every modern city in search of a makeover would like to be measured. The 1992 Olympic Games that it hosted were the most successful of the modern era, and the city became the poster child for urban regeneration and the transformative power of good city planning.

But, arguably, Barcelona became a victim of its own success. As the cruise ships and conventioneers got wise and began to throng into town, Barca's distinctive scene began to become, well, a tad bridge and tunnel. Smarter travellers shifted south to Valencia or across to the Balearics. But they're coming back now, lured by a new breed of hip hotel, the best bar scene in the world, and the now desperately chic Catalan cuisine.

Flooded with EU migrants from France, the Netherlands, Scandinavia and the UK, Barcelona is far more cosmopolitan now than it has ever been, and no longer just Spain's second city or the Catalan capital, but a world-class metropolis. Its already impressive museums have seen the addition of the contemporary art space at the CaixaForum (www.fundacion.lacaixa.es) as well as a no-expense-spared expansion of its great cultural palace the MNAC (www.mnac.es). The familiar art nouveau (or *modernista*) architectural aesthetic is now complemented by a string of new work from a who's who of contemporary international architects. Come to Catalonia; we won't let you put a foot wrong.

ESSENTIAL INFO

FACTS, FIGURES AND USEFUL ADDRESSES

TOURIST OFFICE
Plaça Catalunya 17
T 93 285 3832
www.barcelonaturisme.com

TRANSPORT
Car hire
Avis
T 93 237 5680
www.avis.co.uk
Metro
www.tmb.net
Taxis
Barnataxi
T 93 357 7755

EMERGENCY SERVICES
Ambulance
061
Fire
080
Police
091
24-hour pharmacy
Farmàcia Alvarez
Passeig de Gràcia 26
T 93 302 1124 (night-time only)

CONSULATES
British Consulate
Avinguda Diagonal 477
T 93 366 6200
www.fco.gov.uk
US Consulate
Passeig Reina Elisenda 23
T 93 280 2227
www.barcelona.usconsulate.gov

MONEY
American Express
Plaça Catalunya
T 90 237 5637

POSTAL SERVICES
Post Office
Correu Central
Plaça Antonio López
T 90 219 7197
Shipping
Spain-Tir
T 93 404 2626
www.spaintir.es

BOOKS
Barcelona by Robert Hughes
(Vintage Books USA)
Catalan Cuisine by Colman Andrews
(Harvard Common Press)
Homage To Catalonia by George Orwell
(Penguin Classics)

WEBSITES
Architecture
www.coac.net
www.gaudi2002.bcn.es
Art
www.cccb.org
www.macba.es
www.mnac.es
Newspapers
www.elpais.es
www.lavanguardia.es

COST OF LIVING
**Taxi from airport
to city centre**
£19
Cappuccino
£1.65
Packet of cigarettes
£2.35
Daily newspaper
£0.80
Bottle of champagne
£42

BARCELONA
Area
490 sq km
Population
1.6 million
Currency: euro
€1 = £0.79 = $1.49
Telephone codes
Spain: 34
Barcelona: 93
Time
GMT +1

Paris
Munich
Marseille
Madrid
Barcelona
Rome
SPAIN

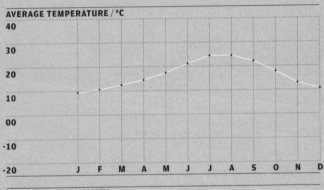

AVERAGE TEMPERATURE / °C

40
30
20
10
00
-10
-20

J F M A M J J A S O N D

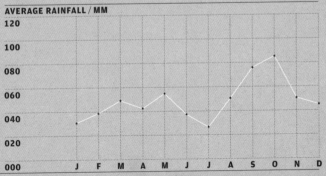

AVERAGE RAINFALL / MM

120
100
080
060
040
020
000

J F M A M J J A S O N D

NEIGHBOURHOODS
THE AREAS YOU NEED TO KNOW AND WHY

To help you navigate the city, we've chosen the most interesting districts (see below and the map inside the back cover) and colour-coded our featured venues, according to their location; those venues that are outside these areas are not coloured.

LA BARCELONETA
The man-made beach created for the 1992 Olympics is the biggest attraction in this robust maritime district. It stands next to the Vila Olímpica, an upscale pleasure ground with many bars and restaurants overlooking the marina, and the luxury Hotel Arts (see p026).

BARRI GÒTIC
The oldest, most atmospheric part of the city, the Gothis Quarter dates back to Roman times. Its winding medieval streets are lorded over by the city's main cathedral.

EL BORN
The Museu Picasso and Museu Tèxtil are both tucked away in El Born's warren of streets. The shopping to be found here is the best in town, although many of the boutiques have now been hijacked by big-name international brands.

L'EIXAMPLE
The name of this district means 'extension' and this is where most of the *modernista* icons can be found, including Gaudí's Casa Batlló (see p044), Casa Milà (see p014) and Sagrada Família (see p045). The elegant Passeig de Gràcia, a power-shopping strip, cuts through the area and the lower pocket near Plaça de la Universitat is known as the 'Gayxample', the city's pink precinct.

GRÀCIA
It is whispered that Gràcia is poised to become the city's next hot area. Boho and pretty, and packed with interesting shops, it has an independent spirit and a friendly, village-type ambience.

POBLE SEC
Residential and laid-back Poble Sec has no major tourist sites, but it is a pleasant place to wander around after visiting the parks and museums of Montjuïc, the city's largest 'green space'.

EL POBLENOU
This area is fast becoming gentrified by upwardly mobile, loft-dwelling creatives and Barceloneses setting up studios in the disused factories and warehouses.

EL RAVAL
Barcelona's largest neighbourhood has seen the most aggressive of the city's gentrification over the years. The upper Raval has swapped its edgy vibe for an arty one, as it's now home to cultural centres MACBA and CCCB (see p042), fashionable bars and trendy boutiques.

SANT PERE
Located just north of trendy El Born, Sant Pere has the stunning Mercat de Santa Caterina (see p010) as its centrepiece.

LANDMARKS

THE SHAPE OF THE CITY SKYLINE

Barcelona is still growing at a dizzying rate. Work over the past decade on the once down-at-heel northern periphery is now coming to an end and its sheer scope has created a 'city within a city'. The Edifici Fòrum 2004 site (see p077), with its keynote building by Herzog & de Meuron, has become a familiar fact of city life (it's now used for large-scale music festivals and cultural events), while Jean Nouvel's Torre Agbar (see p012), the city's flashiest new symbol, anchors the dotcom neighbourhood at the north end of Diagonal. Architects have long since turned their attentions to Barcelona's western flank, and have been busy remodelling it. The construction of the mammoth City of Justice (a new administrative district) is marching along and Richard Rogers (together with his local partners Alonso and Balaguer) is converting Las Arenas, the city's former bullring, into a striking retail-leisure centre. Meanwhile, gentrification of the old city marches on. The Mercat de Santa Caterina (see p010) is the high note of a process that seemingly knows no end.

In the midst of all this upheaval, it can be comforting to cling to the familiar. Casa Milà (see p014) was Gaudí's first purpose-built apartment block and offers a gratifying selection of all his signature riffs for those moments when the summer hawkers and handicams simply infect the Sagrada Família (see p045).

For full addresses, see Resources.

Mercat de Santa Caterina

A redevelopment initiated by Enric Miralles, and completed after his death by his wife, Benedetta Tagliabue, this colourful, wavy-roofed food market was well worth the wait and its £10m cost. The 68 fresh-produce stallholders retained their original signage, but the design made no other concession to tradition. The surrounding streets were widened to set the market in a grander context and to allow natural light to pour in through the 109 irregularly slatted wooden arches that support the roof. The best views of the market and its rooftop mosaics are to be had from atop one of the neighbouring buildings, but the square makes a good reference point for visitors to Sant Pere. *Avinguda de Francesc Cambó 16, www.mercatsantacaterina.net*

Torre Agbar

Jean Nouvel's 142m tower on Diagonal has quickly become a defining feature of Barcelona's skyline. Unless you are a prospective tenant, it's unlikely you'll gain access to the steel-and-glass interior, but it is easy to appreciate the 4,400-windowed tower from Passeig de Gràcia or Plaça de les Glòries Catalanes. Agbar is the local water company, something that Nouvel seldom tires of referencing in the building's design. This rather sensuous structure resembles a bubbling water stream, and its surface appears to ripple under a liquid film. The top floors are clad in clear glass, while below, metal panels descend in tones of white and blue, before being met by the violent orange, fuchsia and red panels that rise from the base. *Plaça de les Glòries Catalanes, www.torreagbar.com*

Monjuïc Communications Tower

It's hard to remember, but there was a time before Santiago Calatrava had built one of his signature towers or bridges in almost every major metropolis. Fittingly, Barcelona was an early proving ground for the Valencia native, who has subsequently become the world's most crowd-pleasing architect after Frank Gehry. His beautiful communications tower, originally built for Telefónica and now renamed Monjuïc Communications Tower, which was based on a sketch the architect made of a kneeling figure making an offering, became the public symbol of the Olympic Park during the 1992 Games. Standing 130m high, it cuts an imposing figure and helps to delineate the Olympic stadium area and the highest point of the mount of Montjuïc itself.

Anella Olímpica, Montjuïc

Casa Milà

Completed in 1910, this purpose-built apartment block, nicknamed La Pedrera (The Stone Quarry), was Gaudí's last civil project before he secluded himself at the site of the Sagrada Família. To build it, Gaudí devised a new way of saving on materials and substituted load-bearing walls for a system of beams and columns. Even the façade, which looks suitably monumental, is actually made up of thin plates of aluminium. This famous wave-like rocky massif has its match inside the building, where right angles are unknown and the appearance is freeform and organic. In reality, all the detail work is painstakingly calculated down to the last millimetre. A visit to the site includes the fascinating Espai Gaudí, a didactic museum on the architect, and an apartment fitted out in the *modernista* décor of his era.
Carrer Provença 261-265,
www.lapedreraeducacio.org

HOTELS

WHERE TO STAY AND WHICH ROOMS TO BOOK

The last few years have seen at least one four- or five-star hotel opening every few months or so, forcing the city's first design-led properties, such as Hotel Claris (Pau Claris 150, T 93 487 6262) and Hotel Arts (see p026) to fight a bit harder to attract a well-heeled clientele. While the former still has a loyal following, thanks to its sharp service ethic, the latter has wisely invested in a complete refurbishment and first-class restaurants, including Arola, the eponymous eaterie of the country's *enfant terrible* of the kitchen, Sergi Arola. Hotel Omm (see p032) has also jumped on the gastro bandwagon with its über-hip restaurant Moo (see p054), as has Hotel Cram (Carrer Aribau 54, T 93 216 7700, www.hotelcram.com), which now has Michelin-awarded chefs running its eateries.

Looking ahead, the design-hotel boom shows no sign of slowing down. In 2007, the five-star AC Miramar (Plaza Carlos Ibáñez 3, T 93 281 1600, www.hotelacmiramar.com), perched on the peak of Montjuïc, opened. On Las Ramblas, historic edifices are rapidly being refitted into luxury hotels. The elegant, colonial-inspired Hotel 1898 (La Rambla 109, T 93 552 9552, www.nnhotels.com) is located in the former Philippine Tobacco Company, while the Hotel Bagués will open in 2008 in an historic palace. The project of a dynasty of jewellers, it will also have an in-house museum displaying its valuable collection of beads and baubles.
For full addresses and room rates, see Resources.

Hotel Axel

The lower left side of L'Eixample district is commonly known as the Gayxample, owing to its abundance of gay bars and clubs. In the middle of it all is the Hotel Axel, the country's first luxury, gay-friendly hotel. Located in a *modernista* building typical of the neighborhood, all 66 rooms, though not terribly spacious, are well lit and well conceived, with king-size beds and a minimum of fussy detailing. (If size is an issue, book one of the superior rooms, which all come with corner balconies.) Even if you are not a guest, the ground-floor bar and restaurant is a good place to network and pick up information on the rather fickle Gayxample scene, while the rooftop Sky Bar is always a hot spot in the summer months.
Carrer Aribau 33, T 93 323 9393, www.hotelaxel.com

Gran Hotel La Florida

Despite being a half-hour drive from the centre of town, this grand property perched on top of Mount Tibidabo is a class act. The rooms are sumptuously furnished with enormous beds and have cavernous marble bathrooms, while the eight designer suites boast unique interiors created by acclaimed artists. The Penthouse Suite was furnished by British artists Ben Jakober and Yannick Yu. Rebecca Horn is responsible for the Tower Terrace Suite and Cristina Macaya has chosen sensual tones for the Tibidabo Suite (above). Dale Keller's Asian-inspired style graces the Japanese Suite, which overlooks one of the hotel's most impressive features, the indoor-outdoor pool (left and overleaf).

Carretera de Vallvidrera al Tibidabo 83-93, T 93 259 3000, www.hotellaflorida.com

Pool, Gran Hotel La Florida

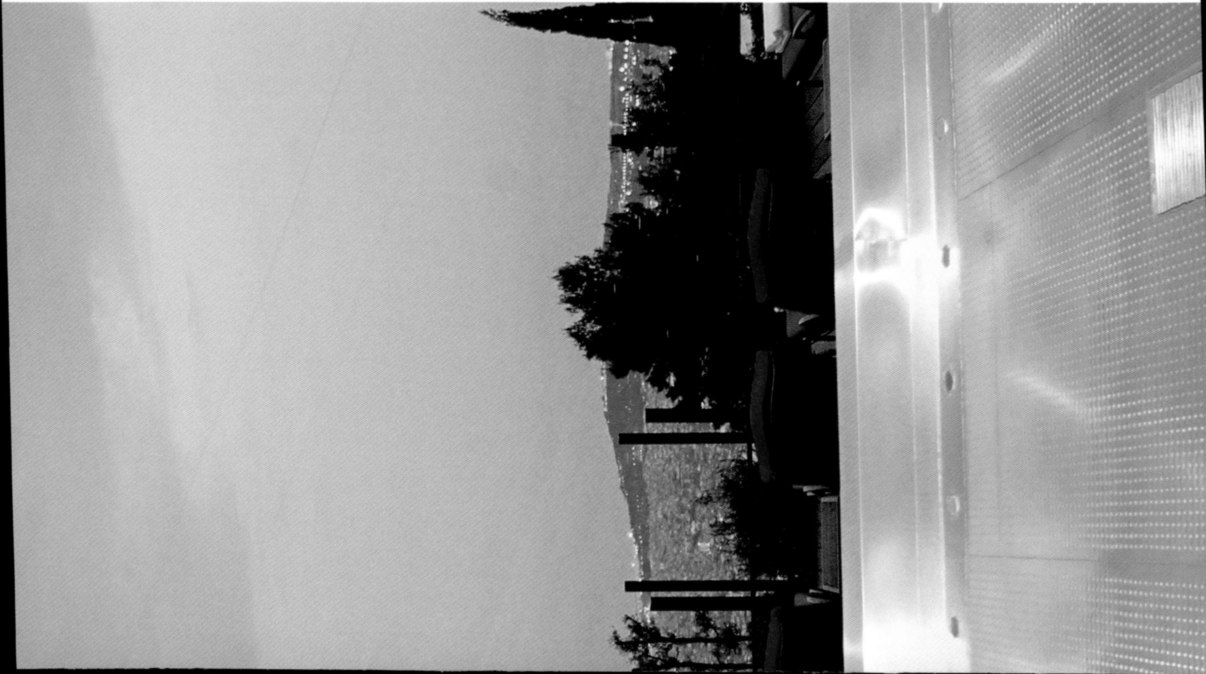

Hotel Diagonal Barcelona

Slick and sexy, the Diagonal is the hotel of choice for the design and architecture aficionado with a big-business expense account (it's in the city's financial district with room rates to match). Built in the shadow of the Torre Agbar (see p012), Catalan architect Juli Capella's interiors complement this already iconic landmark, as the public areas, such as the lobby bar (right), are furnished in a sleek, contemporary style. The rooms have the predictable combination of white linen and dark wood, but are saved by fine finishes, hi-tech facilities and graphic black-and-white prints that serve as headboards. The views are amazing – Rooms 724 and 824 look out onto the Sagrada Família (see p045). The rooftop pool (above) is small, but the sun deck has spectacular vistas.

Avenida Diagonal 205, T 93 489 5300,
www.hoteldiagonalbarcelona.com

Hotel Neri
This bijou 22-room boutique hotel in the heart of Barri Gòtic is utterly charming. Quartzite-clad bathrooms featuring Etro amenities reflect the design philosophy inspired by the five senses. All rooms ending in 01 and 02 look out onto Felip Neri square.
Carrer Sant Sever 5, T 93 304 0655, www.hotelneri.com

Hotel Arts

Built as the flagship hotel for the 1992
Olympics, the 482-room Hotel Arts towers
over the beaches of Barceloneta and
Frank Gehry's flying fish sculpture (right).
Thanks to a refurbishment and its Six
Senses Spa (see p092), Arts is once again
the hotel of choice for smart businessmen,
while its three restaurants have made the
hotel a mecca for foodies. Enoteca serves
regional Spanish dishes, while Bites offers
light meals and snacks round the clock.
The best place to dine is Arola, where
modern interiors harmonise with chef
Sergi Arola's contemporary Spanish tapas.
The hotel's Club rooms come with butler
service, Aqua di Parma toiletries and free
food and drink at the Club Lounge. But
it is the 27 apartments with a personal
concierge service and stunning views
of the city that stand out.
*Carrer de la Marina 19-21, T 93 221 1000,
www.ritzcarlton.com*

Le Méridien Ra Beach Hotel & Spa
If you need a break from Barcelona's
sometimes frenetic pace, drive 40 minutes
south to the Ra Beach Hotel & Spa for
some serious R&R. The thalassotherapy
installation is unequalled, the treatments
sublime, and the food delicious *and*
healthy. The Ra's isolation and discretion
has made it a favourite with film stars,
so try to remain nonchalant if you bump
into Penélope Cruz at check-in.
Avinguda Sanatori 1, Platja de Sant
Salvador, El Vendrell, T 97 769 4200,
www.lemeridien.com

Hesperia Tower

This imposing 107m tower, designed by Richard Rogers, has changed the face of Gran Via, the main route from the airport into Barcelona. Conceived as the centrepiece of the city's new 'financial heart', its five-star hotel starts with the airy lobby (left) and spans 27 floors. There are 280 rooms, including a Presidential Suite on the 26th floor, with a private butler and chauffeur. The amenities (three types of high-speed internet connection, pillow menus and flat-screen TVs) are matched by the excellent Evo restaurant that sits in the glass dome atop the tower. It's headed up by celebrated Michelin-starred Catalan chef Santi Santamaria. *Mare de Déu de Bellvitge 1, T 93 413 5000, www.hesperia-tower.com*

Hotel Omm

The Tragaluz group's first venture into hotels has gone down a storm with the international fashion set, and the city's beautiful people are often to be found draped over the 1950s-inspired furniture in the lounge bar (right). The dark corridors leading to the rooms upstairs feel like futuristic catwalks, thanks to strips of lighting set into the floor. Balconies are ingeniously tucked behind panels of the hotel's façade (above), which looks as if it has been peeled back; those balconies in Rooms 501 and 601 offer views of Casa Milà (see p014). The rooftop pool, the Spaciomm spa, with its bespoke products and acclaimed in-house hair salon New Look, cater to the preened and the terminally hip; as does the surprisingly well-equipped basement club Ommsession.
Carrer Rosselló 265, T 93 445 4000, www.hotelomm.es

Casa Camper

True to the philosophy of the quirky shoe company that owns it, Casa Camper is eco-friendly (everything is recycled), health-conscious and incredibly urban. Guests can rent the bicycles dangling from the roof in the entrance and whizz round El Raval, having planned their route with the maps mounted in the mini-lounge that comes with each room. The architects have cleverly overcome the split layout of the building by creating a green wall of potted plants in the light well (left), which creates a pleasantly verdant vista. There's no room service, but the striking self-service café (above), which is open only to guests, serves snacks 24 hours a day.
Carrer Elisabets 11, T 93 342 6280, www.casacamper.com

Hotel Pulitzer

Located a stone's throw from the Plaça Catalunya, the city's main hub, and Las Ramblas, the Hotel Pulitzer has 91 rooms, which make up for their lack of floor space with fabulously eclectic interiors. Each room has a marble bathroom, with sunken tub and slate floors, but try to reserve Rooms 306 or 506, which feature leather sofas, high ceilings and balconies. Despite its bijou size, the Pulitzer really packs a punch and was one of the first urban hotels to create a bar scene. The lobby bar (right) hosts Visit, a cocktail bar-café that serves substantial snacks and drinks until midnight. In the summer months, a host of trendy Barceloneses take the glass lift to Visit Up, a rooftop bar and restaurant with fabulous views of the city's skyline.
Carrer de Bergara 8, T 93 481 6767, www.hotelpulitzer.es

Hotel 54

Located in the former HQ of the local fishing guild, the bijou Hotel 54 is the strongest sign that the winds of change are sweeping through the gritty beachside *barri* of Barceloneta. The rooms' interiors, with velvet headboards, bright textiles and slate floors, are pleasant enough. But the clincher is the curtain glass window that offers a staggering view of the harbour and beyond. (Specify you want a port-side room when booking, or try your luck on Room 404, the largest standard with vistas of both sea and street.) For non-guests, Hotel 54 offers the basement Suite Royale nightclub (see p058) and a rooftop bar, which is a stunning place to watch the sun set behind Montjuïc. *Passeig Joan de Borbó 54, T 93 225 0054*

Hotel Soho

Alfredo Arribas's Soho stands out among the plethora of Barcelona's new breed of design hotels. Decorative frippery has been forsaken for details that actually work, like user-friendly, intelligent lighting that can match your mood, and furniture that can be easily moved around to suit your needs. The rear rooms look out onto one of L'Eixample's typical interior *patis* (book a corner room ending in a 2 or 4 for a slightly larger space) and many have wood-decked terraces (if yours doesn't, head to the rooftop terrace and plunge pool). The public areas feature an inspired mix of textures in burnt colors and op-art installations, and the façade itself pulsates at night with the soft glow of multicoloured backlights.
Gran Via 543-545, T 93 552 9610, www.nnhotels.es

24 HOURS

SEE THE BEST OF THE CITY IN JUST ONE DAY

Barcelona has such a bewildering range of striking architecture and world-class museums that, on a first visit, even the most organised visitor can only hope to scratch the surface. If you're more interested in the city's heritage than in its architecture and contemporary art, skip MACBA (Plaça dels Angels, T 93 412 0810, www.macba.es) and CCCB (see p042) in El Raval and head for El Born, where the Museu Picasso (Carrer Montcada 15-23, T 93 236 3000, www.museupicasso.bcn.es) charts the evolution of the painter's oeuvre. Hop across the street to the Museu Tèxtil (Carrer Montcada 12-14, T 93 319 7603, www.museutextil.bcn.es), where the shop sells great gadgets and one-off garments and the courtyard café serves an excellent light lunch.

Then head for Montjuïc, where you'll find the Fundació Joan Miró (Parc de Montjuïc, T 93 443 0470, www.bcn.fjmiro.es) and the Mies van der Rohe Pavilion (see p074), a seminal building designed to showcase German design and the 'Barcelona' chair. Across the road, the CaixaForum (Avinguda del Marquès de Comillas 6-8, T 93 476 8600, www.fundacio.lacaixa.es) exhibits cutting-edge shows doing the rounds of Europe. Afterwards, relax in front of the Font Màgica de Montjuïc (Plaça d'Espanya, open 8pm-midnight, May to September, 7-9pm, October to April), an extravaganza of water jets that dance to Tchaikovsky and Abba. *For full addresses, see Resources.*

09.00 Cuines Santa Caterina

Start the day with a croissant, pastry or *pan con tomate* and *café con leche* at upmarket cantina Cuines Santa Caterina (breakfast served from 8-11.30am). The menus are the placemats, on which dishes are divided into their base ingredients and origin on a bingo-like grid. The food arrives in no particular order, adding to the relaxed informality of the place. All the products used have been sourced from the Mercat de Santa Caterina (see p010) that the restaurant calls home, so the Cuines is a perfect introduction to the delicacies on offer. After breakfast, stock up on condiments, chorizos and olive oil, and admire the playfulness of the architecture around you – designed by the late Enric Miralles.
Avinguda Francesc Cambó 16, T 93 268 9918, www.mercatsantacaterina.net

11.00 CCCB
The CCCB acts as a lively cultural centre and venue for the city's endless round of art, music and other festivals and sits next door to the Richard Meier-designed modern art museum MACBA. Opposite is the Foment de les Arts Decoratives (FAD), where the city's vibrant design community hang out and take lunch at the excellent FADfood (T 93 443 7520). *Montalegre 5, T 93 306 4100, www.cccb.org*

15.00 Casa Batlló

After lunch, head north to the elegant Passeig de Gràcia, where you'll come across the Manzana de Discòrdia (block of discord), home to three key *modernista* buildings. The centerpiece (and the only one fully open to the public) is the Casa Batlló, one of Gaudí's most distinctive (and crowd-pleasing) structures. Its extraordinary *trencadis* (broken tile) mosaic which blankets the façade is mesmerising, but you'll probably be more taken aback by the surreal, undulating interiors. Highlights include the drawing room with its superb stained glass windows and sinuous frames, the snake-like stairwell and the shimmering, tile-clad roof, said to represent the dragon slain by Catalonia's patron saint, Sant Jordi.

Passeig de Gràcia 43, T 93 216 0306, www.casabatllo.es

17.00 Sagrada Família

Love it or loathe it, Gaudí's cathedral has become *the* architectural icon of the city, despite the fact that it is unfinished a century on and likely to remain so for at least another 40 years. Take the lift up one of the 18 towers to admire the blobby spires, wander through the crypt where Gaudí's tomb is and the museum with his upside-down mirrored maquettes, then step outside. The highly-detailed Nativity façade was finished by Gaudí, but the Passion façade, with its square-headed apostles and crucified Christ (a work of local sculptor Josep Subirachs) caused a storm of criticism when it was unveiled in the 1980s, leading many to opine that construction should have died when the great architect did.
Carrer de Mallorca 401, T 93 207 3031, www.sagradafamilia.org

20.30 Sugar Club

After a well-earned siesta, jump into a cab and head to the Sugar Club, a nightclub, lounge and cocktail bar that opens at 8pm. Located in the city's World Trade Center, it offers some of the best views in town and is the ideal spot for a preprandial sundowner (Spaniards wouldn't dream of having dinner until 9.30pm at the very earliest). If you like the vibe here, come back after eating, when the resident DJs, David Mas and Gustavo Sosa, open up the club and lounge at 11pm. By midnight, both start to fill up with Barcelona's beautiful people. *World Trade Center, T 93 508 8325, www.sugarclub-barcelona.com*

22.00 Il Giardinetto

Uptown in both vibe and location, Il Giardinetto is a classic eaterie favoured by the city's creative establishment. Owned by the same couple as Flash Flash (see p049), and winner of a major design award at the height of the 1980s *disseny* fever, the service is sharp and the interiors have lost none of their appeal. The banquettes are teal coloured and the supporting columns have been painted to resemble trees, with canopies of leaves covering the ceiling, which is lovingly retouched each year. As the name suggests, the food is Italian. Order the baked brie with marmalade of tomato and apple, followed by *penne alla Sophia Loren*.
Carrer Granada del Penedès 22,
T 93 218 7536

URBAN LIFE

CAFÉS, RESTAURANTS, BARS AND NIGHTCLUBS

As well as its *modernista* architecture, Barcelona has developed its own contemporary Catalan cuisine thanks to the runaway success of El Bullí (Cala Montjoi, T 97 215 0457; open from April to October only and book at least a year in advance), two hours north on the Costa Brava. Chef Ferran Adrià has embraced science, alchemy and aroma to create a cuisine that has earned the restaurant a reputation as one of the best in the world. Predictably, many local start-ups have tried to copy his formula, with varying success. A couple of the better ones include Comerç 24 (Carrer Comerç 24, T 93 319 2102), run by an ex Bullí chef, and Santa María (Carrer Comerç 17, T 93 315 1227, www.santamaria.biz). More conservative palates should stick to classic venues that serve traditional fare, such as 7 Portes (Passeig d'Isabel II 14, T 93 319 3033) and Can Ravell (Carrer Aragó 313, T 93 457 5114, www.ravell.com).

Art aficionados can combine a visit to the Museu Picasso with a meal or coffee at Els 4 Gats (Carrer Montsió 3, T 93 302 4140), which was frequented by the artist at the beginning of the last century. This is where Picasso picked up his first commission, designing the still-in-use menu, and a handful of his early sketches adorn the walls. Fans of Gaudí should reserve a table at the excellent Casa Calvet (Carrer de Casp 48, T 93 412 4012, www.casacalvet.es), which is housed in another distinctive building by the architect. *For full addresses, see Resources.*

Flash Flash

Owned by top 1970s fashion photographer Leopoldo Pomés, this cheap but chic *tortilleria* is a classic, and remains a favourite haunt for Barcelonians of all ages. Take a seat at one of the white leatherette banquettes and admire the walls adorned with stencilled images of Pomés' wife, Karin Leiz. Barcelona's answer to Twiggy, Leiz strikes various poses while brandishing a camera whose flash morphs into the café's light fittings. Tortillas are the house speciality (there are around 50 variations, including sweet ones), but for egg-shy diners the menu offers a selection of burgers, the best of which is the Cadillac Hamburger. Open until 1am, the restaurant is an excellent choice for a late-night supper.
Carrer Granada del Penedès 25,
T 93 237 0990

Torre d'Alta Mar
Slick interiors and a 360-degree view of the city and the Med make this Barceloneta fish restaurant, housed 75m up in a former cable-car tower, a favourite with the smoother sort of businessmen and courting couples. Ask for a corner table and order the *suquet*, a Catalan-style bouillabaisse. *Passeig Joan de Borbò 88, T 93 221 0007, www.torredealtamar.com*

Tapioles 53

In a city awash with trendified restaurants serving up molecular, morsel-sized servings, Tapioles 53 is a rare breed. It functions as a gastro-club, meaning there are no walk-ins and no lengthy menu to plough through. Instead, Australian chef Sarah Stothart will reel off the day's three-course set menu once you take a seat. It changes weekly, but be assured you will be dining on the best of the Med's dishes with a few exotic Asian specialities thrown in. Stothart learned her craft from her mother (a supreme cook and gastronome), and her father's abstract oil paintings of the El Penedés vineyards adorn the high walls of this old umbrella factory, making dinner at Tapioles 53 a highly personal and intimate experience. *Carrer Tapioles 53, T 93 329 2238, www.tapioles53.com*

Cinc Sentits

Chef Jordi Artal and maître d' Amelia Artal are the charming brother-and-sister team who run this L'Eixample restaurant, which serves modern Catalan cuisine in elegant surroundings. If you want to place yourself in the chef's hands, try the tasting menu, offered in long or short form, which comes with a wine pairing for each course. If you order à la carte, the foie gras with vinegar-glazed leeks, and lamb cutlets with porcini crust come highly recommended. The Iberian suckling pig served with apples poached in *vi ranci* is another highlight. Cinc Sentits is gaining a worldwide reputation for its excellent food, so book well in advance. *Carrer d'Aribau 58, T 93 323 9490, www.cincsentits.com*

Moo

Awarded a Michelin star at the end of 2005, Moo is run by the Roca brothers, who propelled the Girona restaurant El Celler de Can Roca to two-star status in 2002. The ground floor of Hotel Omm (see p032) provides a suitably hip setting for this venture, which offers a mix of the sublime, namely a wonderful Catalan tasting menu, and the silly – puddings that are named after famous perfumes.
Carrer Rosselló 265, T 93 445 4000

Mondo

Seemingly conceived to provide a nocturnal playground for the growing community of yacht dwellers in Port Vell, Mondo is located on Maremagnum, a pleasure-plex on an artificial island in the sea. After a seafood dinner in the restaurant overlooking the marina, the cashed-up and carefree head indoors to dance the night away in the pop art-meets-*The Jetsons* red-and-white interior or canoodle in the private Krug room, painted green and rotund like the champagne's distinctive bottle. If you don't have a yacht to park outside, call ahead for their Hummer chauffeur service and at least arrive in overland style.
Moll D'Espanya s/n, T 93 221 3911, www.mondobcn.com

Suite Royale
After the new Hotel 54 opened near the
beach (see p038), the much mourned Café
Royale – a sophisticated club banished
from the old town by the city's new 'civility'
laws – was relocated to the basement
under its new name, Suite Royale. The
same boudoir-inspired décor as the old
venue applies, as does the jazz-fusion
sounds spun by resident DJ Fred Guzzo.
Drop by on a Tuesday or Wednesday
for a rare opportunity to hear live jazz
in an intimate setting.
Passeig Joan de Borbó 54, T 93 225 7038

Cata 1.81

This tiny gourmet tapas bar, which has bright, slightly stark interiors, has proved a huge hit with trendy locals. 'Cata' means 'tasting', and when the restaurant first opened, the wine list of around 250 bottles was the main draw, especially for oenophiles looking to sample as many 25cl decanters as possible. More recently, the wine list has been scaled down and the tapas, such as salt cod with peppers, or fried tuna with caramelised watermelon, are now served as *platillos* – dishes designed to be shared. Be warned, the menu is in Catalan only, and the waiting staff tend to be too busy to translate. It's definitely worth a visit, though.
Carrer València 181, T 93 323 6818

Noti

This sophisticated L'Eixample eaterie is located in what was the HQ of a major (and hugely popular) newspaper. The literati flocked back when it reopened as Noti, a dramatic space designed by Francesc Pons and inspired by *la corrida* (the bullfight). Decked out in red, black and hot pink, there is an upbeat, energetic atmosphere in the place to match. The food is modern European (try the rich fish soup, lobster carpaccio or seared tuna) and the wine list is well chosen and well priced. If you're still there several hours later, you may be joined by a trendy DJ or two. Noti becomes a favourite haunt of the city's beautiful people late into the night, so it's a good place to see and be seen, and perhaps spot a few celebs.
Carrer Roger de Llúria 35, T 93 342 6673, www.noti-universal.com

Ottimo

This Italian restaurant, which opened in 2005, has an old-school 1950s elegance, thanks to interiors by Francesc Pons and the Sinatra soundtrack that plays while you dine. Well-heeled locals feast on well-executed modern Italian cuisine with Catalan accents. The menu changes seasonally, but you should certainly try the rigatoni Josep Carreras or tagliatelle with truffle oil and poached eggs. For an intimate meal, book a corner table, or if you want to watch the world go by, reserve table three, which looks out onto the street. The bar staff at Ottimo mix a mean cocktail, so we recommend starting your evening with a bellini or two.
Enric Granados 95, T 93 217 1310,
www.ottimorestaurants.com

Inopia Classic Bar

This tapas bar in an off-the-radar pocket of L'Eixample has become a runaway success. Inopia is the brainchild of Albert Adrià (brother of Ferran), but don't expect any molecular trickery. A child of the suburbs, Adrià wished to recreate the tapas haunts of his youth, thus the distinctive tiling, blackboard menu, zinc bar and strip lighting. *Carrer Tamarit 104, T 93 424 5231*

Gimlet

This tiny, long-established bar sees
trendy rivals come and go, but remains
one of El Born's classic destinations.
Gimlet serves delicious eponymous
gin-and-lime cocktails, with numerous
inventive variations created by the
highly skilled barmen. It attracts a
fashionable crowd of locals and in-the-
know foreigners and gets absolutely
packed at the weekend, so we recommend
calling in on a quieter Wednesday night.
This is a classy establishment that you
should visit at least once while in town.
Carrer del Rec 24, T 93 310 1027

Dry Martini

Many *coctelerías* dot the grid of the L'Eixample district, but Dry Martini has remained the leader of the pack for nearly 40 years. Although it's located on the ground floor of a 1980s apartment block, the décor is pure speakeasy: leather sofas form cosy conversation pits and liveried mixers wait behind the mahogany bar with shakers in hand. It's a favourite with the city's intelligentsia, who make a beeline post-work (around 8.30pm) for a de-stressing *cubata* (mixed drink). After dinner the scene is more lively, with patrons of all stripes piling in after eating at one of the nearby restaurants. *Carrer Aribau 162-166, T 93 217 5072, www.drymartinibcn.com*

Negroni

After decades of wearing its grunge label loud and proud, El Raval's bar-hopping stretch, the Carrer Joaquim Costa, is starting to sprout some stylish alternatives. One of the best is the tiny *coctelería* Negroni. Locals cram in just before midnight, either settling in (if lucky) onto the lone sofa downstairs or elbowing each other at the front bar, a retro, glass-topped design etched with a 1950s motif. As the name (and overhanging chandeliers made of those distinctive squat bottles) suggest, Negroni specialises in Campari-based cocktails, though really there is nothing that this bar's able mixers can't concoct.
Carrer Joaquim Costa 46, T 661 361 067

INSIDER'S GUIDE

ALEX AL-BADER, MODEL

Alex Al-Bader's modelling career has taken her around the world, from Tokyo to London, but she always finds time to return to her native Barcelona. Her favourite breakfast spot is the market stall Bar Pinotxo (La Boqueria 466-467, La Rambla 91, T 93 317 1731), at the entrance to La Boqueria market. When wandering around Barri Gòtic, she suggests stopping for a coffee at either of the two cafés in Plaça del Pi. Her favourite spots for lunch include Cal Pep (Plaça de les Olles 8, T 93 310 7961, www.calpep.com) in El Born, which serves delicious tapas, good fillet of beef and sea bass, and the small but atmospheric El Lobito (Ginebra 9, T 93 319 9164) in Barceloneta, which offers seasonal seafood for lunch or dinner.

Al-Bader likes to spend her evenings in Barceloneta, calling in at El Vaso de Oro (Balboa 6, T 93 319 3098) for tapas, followed by dinner at Agua (Passeig Marítim 30, T 93 225 1272), and then cocktails next door at Cdlc (Passeig Marítim 32, T 93 224 0470). Her favourite clubs are Otto Zutz (Carrer Lincoln 15, T 93 238 0722, www.ottozutz.com), Hotel Omm's (see p032) hip basement club Ommsession (Carrer Rosselló 265, T 93 445 4000) and Oven (Carrer Ramón Turró 124-126, T 93 221 0602), which is in the revamped industrial district of El Poblenou. If you arrive at Oven in the early evening, have dinner in the restaurant, and if you're visiting in the summer, ask for a table on the terrace.

For full addresses, see Resources.

ARCHITOUR

A GUIDE TO BARCELONA'S ICONIC BUILDINGS

Barcelona is in the midst of a long and intense love affair with architecture. It has been here before, of course. The big difference is that a century or so ago its affections were directed at one man, the extraordinary Antoni Gaudí. Today, the city is more profligate with its affections. A single urban regeneration programme – the scheme at Diagonal Mar – attracted the talents of Jean Nouvel, EMBT, Herzog & de Meuron, Dominique Perrault, innovative Dutch architects MVRDV and Josep Lluis Mateo.

Still, a trip to the city would be incomplete without a mini Gaudí tour: Sagrada Família (see p045), Casa Milà (see p014) and Casa Batlló (see p044), for instance. But if Gaudí's frilly, faux art nouveau isn't to your taste, there are now other options. A visit to Taller de Arquitectura (opposite) might help make more sense of them. Neither a part of Barcelona's fin-de-siècle architectural past nor a beneficiary of the pre- and post-Olympic Games redevelopment frenzies, it's perhaps been a little neglected. But, in a way, it showcases the lesson that Barcelona has learned over the years. A local architect spent two years remodelling a disused cement factory, and demonstrated in the process the story of today's Barcelona. It's a story of how ambitious architecture, such as Torre Agbar (see p012), Mercat de Santa Caterina (see p010) and Edifici Fòrum (see p077), can illuminate the road to reinvention. *For full addresses, see Resources.*

Taller de Arquitectura

A Barcelona native, the architect Ricardo Bofill has built up a practice that produces successful, sophisticated, if seldom heart-stopping, designs all over the world, from a head office for Cartier in Paris to a conference centre in China. For a peek at the firm's idealist past, the cultural centre that serves as its HQ is hard to beat. A remarkable conversion of an abandoned local cement works, which was completed in 1975, with more than 30 silos, acres of machine rooms and disused subterranean galleries, the Taller de Arquitectura was conceived as a place where philosophers, engineers, writers and film-makers could all hang out and solve the problems of the city. Amazingly, the grandeur of this space does justice to the wildness of that dream. *Sant Just Desvern 14, T 93 449 9900, www.bofill.com*

Mies van der Rohe Pavilion

This iconic monument to rationalism, which was built as the German Pavilion for the 1929 Barcelona International Exhibition, became a milestone in modern European architecture. All marble, onyx, chrome and glass, it is the true home of Mies van der Rohe's 'Barcelona' chair. The pavilion was disassembled in 1930, but in 1980, Oriol Bohigas, then head of urban planning at Barcelona City Council, began to appoint a team to research, design and oversee its reconstruction. Ignasi de Solà-Morales, Cristian Cirici and Fernando Ramos were the appointed architects. Work began in 1983 and the new building was opened on its original site in 1986.
Avinguda del Marquès de Comillas, T 93 423 4016, www.miesbcn.com

Torre de Collserola

Of all the infrastructural improvements wrought by the 1992 Olympics, few were more important to the city's looks in the long term than Foster and Partners' TV tower on Mount Tibidabo. Without the games, there's little doubt that the hill would now be awash with radio masts and TV aerials. Fortunately, the television companies were prevailed upon to combine forces and share this little engineering marvel. Foster managed to house the 288m-high tower on a slender base just 4.5m across. The result is that, while the observation deck offers great views of Barcelona, the view of the tower from the city is almost as spectacular.
Carretera de Vallvidrera al Tibidabo,
T 93 406 9354, www.torredecollserola.com

Edifici Fòrum

Herzog & de Meuron's contribution to the city's vast northern redevelopment, this edifice was purpose built for the huge site that hosted Fòrum 2004, a year-long cycle of debates and conferences. The cobalt-blue building was conceived as a sponge, with water running down its concrete walls, both to reinforce the image and to provide an environmentally friendly cooling system. Criticised for its cost, Fòrum 2004 never became the groundbreaking event the city's authorities were hoping for. The site is now mainly used for festivals and you are free to wander around it (seek out Beth Gali's charming, landscaped Zona de Banys near the waterfront). For an interior view of Herzog & de Meuron's work, book a table at Klein (T 93 356 3088), a haute cuisine restaurant inside the pavilion itself. *Parc Fòrum, Rambla Prim 1*

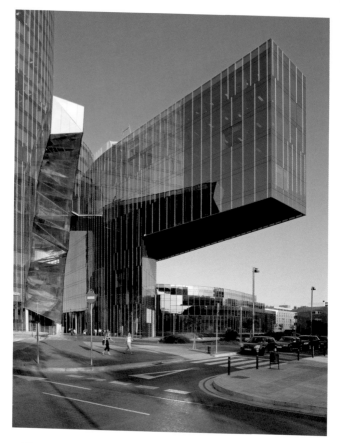

Edifici Gas Natural

Like the Mercat de Santa Caterina (see p010), architect Benedetta Tagliabue saw through the completion of the Edifici Gas Natural, the new HQ of the local gas supplier, after her husband and working partner Enric Miralles' untimely death in 2000. Standing at the crossroads between Barceloneta, the old maritime district and the modern Vila Olímpica, this brave new building is a sum of various parts; an 86m-high tower, a 40m-long annexe (nicknamed the 'aircraft carrier') cantilvering off the side and a four-storey axis in between (we suggest viewing the work from all sides in order to understand its complicated geometry). Its curtain glass façade acts as a mirror for the surrounding skyscapers, including the Hotel Arts (see p026).

Plaça del Gas 1

Diagonal Mar Park

Initially bitterly controversial, the passage of time and the greening of the site has now made EMBT's park a firm local favourite. It helps that their treatment clearly harks back to the work of the city's favourite son. And while the design of Gaudi's Park Güell arguably dominates its function, here the architecture takes a back seat to a fabulous open space located where the Avinguda Diagonal meets the sea. The park itself consists of six areas, with separate sections for dogs, sports, children and so on, all grouped around the water, which cuts through the site and is punctuated by the architects' remarkable fountains.

Avinguda Diagonal y Cinturón Ronda Litoral, www.diagonalmar.com

SHOPPING
THE BEST RETAIL THERAPY AND WHAT TO BUY

A trip to any cultural or culinary hotspot in Barcelona should always be combined with some targeted retail therapy, as all its main districts have a great selection of specialist boutiques. El Born is best for fashion and designer objects. Head to the warren of streets running off the Passieg del Born, particularly Como Agua de Mayo (Carrer Argenteria 43, T 93 319 2330) for womenswear (seek out handmade shoes by Chie Mihara) and Lobby (Carrer Ribera 5, T 93 319 3855, www.lobby-bcn.com) for men's and women's clothes and accessories, especially its in-house label. Uptown, Castañer (Carrer Mestre Nicolau 23, T 93 414 2428) has been making high-quality, newly fashionable espadrilles for decades – Yves Saint Laurent featured them in his collections back in the 1970s.

Foodies can stock up on myriad local delicacies at the excellent supermarket in the basement of El Corte Ingles department store (Plaça de Catalunya 14, T 93 306 3800); wine buffs should head to Lavinia (Diagonal 605, T 93 363 4445) for a good choice of regional Spanish numbers. La Central (Carrer Elisabets 6, T 93 317 0293) in El Raval is one of the biggest and best bookshops in town. For a more specialised array of tomes on art, design and youth culture, walk round the corner to Ras (Carrer del Doctor Dou 10, T 93 412 7199). For literature on architecture, particularly books on Gaudí, the shop at Casa Milà (see p014) is excellent.
For full addresses, see Resources.

Coquette

One of the better boutiques in El Born, Barcelona's haven of hip, Coquette is located in a large corner locale with a soothing interior that falls just the right side of retro. An old atelier feel has been cleverly created with stripped back, turned wood tables, exposed brick, velvet drapes and OTT shell chandeliers as a quirky high note. Owner Isabel Gonzalez Campelo has hand-selected hard-to-get European talent, such as the Canadian-born, Paris-based Tara Jarmon, Isabel Marant, Chloe's cult label See and the up-and-coming Masscob from Galicia. Exotic enamel jewellery from Raquel Moreno adorns the central table, alongside flasks of unique artisan candles and perfumes.
Calle Rec 65, T 93 319 2976,
www.coquettebcn.com

Xocoa
The success of this family-run business
of funky chocolate boutiques seemingly
knows no bounds. Xocoa wraps its
unusual flavours, which include saffron
and lavender, into colourful, pop-art
packaging, making them great gifts to
pop into your hand luggage. The calorie
conscious can go for a new range of
chocolate-based body products.
Carrer Petritxol 11-13, T 93 301 1197,
www.xocoa-bcn.com

Vinçon

Barcelona's premier design emporium since the 1960s, Vinçon spans three floors, boasts its own art gallery, roof terrace for garden furniture – offering unique vistas of the Casa Milá (see p014), next door – and show apartment for exhibiting furniture. The window displays are never less than show-stopping, but inside a huge panorama of home and office wear is laid out without ceremony, casually mixing the humble and high-end with carefree panache. If you are looking for an iconic piece to take home, head for the lighting department to snap up the reinterpretation of the modernist 'Cesta' light (above), £375. Designed by Miguel Milá, the light has a cherrywood frame and opal-white glass shade.
Passeig de Gràcia 96, T 93 215 6050, www.vincon.com

Iguapop

This spacious, whitewashed gallery in El Born, an offshoot of a major company of music promoters, blurs the lines between art, graphics and design. Shows, which generally open on a Thursday evening and draw in the doyens of the city's counterculture, range from the kittenish images of local graffiti artist Miss Van, Tim Biskup's bright, cartoon-like creations and the neo-baroque ceramics of Jaime Hayon. The shop sells a selection of smaller objects by their represented artists, as well as a range of cult-status street and club wear and accessories. *Carrer Comerç 15, T 93 310 0735 (gallery), T 93 319 6813 (shop), www.iguapop.net*

Maxalot

Dutch couple Max Akkerman and Lotje Sodderland's groovy gallery is based on the original concept of elevating graphics and graffiti into an artform by producing colourful, abstract wallpaper that is as much a feature in a room as the furniture. Located in the heart of Barri Gòtic, this small space is devoted to exhibitions of work by some of the world's most cutting-edge creatives. If an image or particular wallpaper catches your eye, a made-to-measure order can be produced. One of our favourite designs is the 'Fuji One' wallpaper (above), from £250 per sq m, by the French art director and illustrator Pier Fichefeux.

Carrer Palma de Sant Just 9, T 93 310 1066, www.maxalot.com

SPORTS AND SPAS
WORK OUT, CHILL OUT OR JUST WATCH

Spain's most popular sport is undoubtedly football, and Barcelona is even more enamoured of the beautiful game due to its two Primera Liga teams. Tickets to watch FC Barcelona (T 902 189 900, www.fcbarcelona.com) are like gold dust, but you'll have better luck getting seats to watch the less famous Espanyol (Estadi Olímpic 17-19, www.rcdespanyol.com). Thanks to the 1992 Olympics, the city is well serviced for sports, hosting 17 international events every year, the most famous of which is the Spanish Grand Prix (Circuit de Catalunya, Montmeló, T 93 571 9708), when almost all of the hotels in town are sold out.

Barcelona's city beaches are packed in summer, but they are the perfect spot for an early-morning jog or a stroll before the sun-worshippers descend. Start at Barceloneta beach and follow the boardwalk to the Hotel Arts (see p026) and onto the Fòrum complex to admire Herzog & de Meuron's distinctive pavilion (see p077). If the heat is too stifling, head for Carretera de les Aigües in Tibidabo for fresh mountain air and unrivalled views. Thanks to the new bike-share service, Bicing, urban cycling has taken off in a big way. Bikes can be hired at most tourist offices and come with a map of city cycle routes. Alternatively, Bike Rental Barcelona (T 666 057 655, www.bikerentalbarcelona.com) can deliver the latest models, including folding bikes, directly to your hotel.
For full addresses, see Resources.

O2 Centro Wellness

This centre for fitness, beauty and wellness is state of the art, and marries excellent facilities with slick interiors, courtesy of architects Luis Alonso and Sergio Balaguer. Many of its spaces have magnificent views of the Parc de Quinta Amelia, most notably the pool, which is clad in black slate in the distinctive style of Peter Zumthor's celebrated spa in Vals, Switzerland. As well as all the usual spa facilities, O2 offers a wide range of cardiovascular programmes and a well-designed, tailored programme for back problems that aims to cure through preventative exercise. You can even bring your children, get your laundry done, have a haircut, grab a healthy lunch and do a spot of tai chi. A day pass is £37.
Carrer Eduardo Conde 2-6, T 93 205 3976, www.o2centrowellness.com

Centre Internacional de Tennis
Serious, semi-professional players
affiliated with the International Tennis
Federation should set their sights on
the Centre Internacional de Tennis, which
has 35 courts and offers specialised
technical, tactical and physical training,
on-site physiotherapy, sports massage
and even accommodation. The more
casual alternative is the Vall Parc Tennis
Club (T 93 212 6789), which is next to Gran

Hotel La Florida (see p019) in Tibidabo.
It has 13 courts, as well as squash, a
gym and a pool.
Carrer Verge de Montserrat, T 93 567 7500,
centreinternacional.fctennis.org

Six Senses Spa
Located in the Hotel Arts (see p026), in terms of location, this spa is hard to beat. On offer are a plethora of treatments, including chromotherapy and three-hour pampering packages. Book well ahead as guests are given preference.
Carrer de la Marina 19-21, T 93 224 7067, www.sixsenses.com

Llobregat Sports Centre
Barcelona's well served for swimmers;
head to Piscines Picornell (T 93 423 4041)
for serious lengths or Club Natació-
Atletic (T 93 221 0010) for indoor or
outdoor bathing and a beachside
terrace. Most spectacular, though, is
Alvaro Siza's pool at Llobregat Sports
Centre, with its 62 circular skylights
set in a domed concrete roof.
*Carrer Mossèn Jacint Verdaguer 16-18,
T 93 377 5454, www.cornellaweb.com*

ESCAPES

WHERE TO GO IF YOU WANT TO LEAVE TOWN

Although Barcelona's beaches and the park in Montjuïc provide some respite from the noise and traffic of the city, a day in the countryside or the Costa Brava will offer a welcome breather. A trip to the Teatre-Museu Dalí in Figueres (Plaça Gala-Salvador Dalí 5, T 97 267 7500, www.salvador-dali.org) can be combined with a visit to the charming seaside village of Cadaqués (see p100), where you can also view the artist's private home. Just ten minutes north of the city, Collserola is the city's rural playground, and many head here for a day's cycling or walking. The mountains and monastery of Montserrat (www.abadiamontserrat.net) are a must for pilgrims, nature lovers and rock climbers, while Tarragona, only an hour south of Barcelona by train, has extensive Roman ruins and was declared a World Heritage Site in 2000.

If you need some sea air, head south to Sitges (opposite) or north to San Pol de Mar. Inland and just an hour north by train from the Passieg de Gràcia station, the handsome town of Girona (see p101) boasts a fine medieval quarter and its surrounding countryside has many untouched villages and little-known gems such as the hotel Mas de Torrent (Afores de Torrent, T 90 255 0321). During winter, the Vall de Nuria (www.valldenuria.com) offers perfect skiing, and the resort has ten slopes, glaciers and a ski school. Take a train from Barcelona's Sants station to Ribes de Freser, then the *cremallera*. *For full addresses, see Resources*.

Sitges

This charming resort beloved by Barceloneses and holidaying gays of all nationalities is only a scenic 25-minute train journey from the Passeig de Gràcia or Sants train station. Get there early to guarantee a decent space on the beach, then, after a morning of sun, go for a light lunch at the excellent Al Fresco (T 93 894 0600) before spending the afternoon wandering through the town's winding streets and stopping off at the Cau Ferrat Museum (T 93 894 0364), the former home of the flamboyant *modernista* painter Santiago Rusiñol. Enjoy dinner at the sea-facing Tambucho (T 93 894 7912) before catching the last train back to Barcelona.

Bodega Codorníu, El Penedés

El Penedés is Catalunya's wine country, and its most famous vineyard is Bodega Codorníu, a rambling estate designed by *modernista* master architect Josep Puig i Cadafalch. Book ahead for a tour and enjoy sampling the excellent reds, whites and cavas it produces. The capital of the region is Vilafranca (an hour from Barcelona's Sants station), a bustling provincial town that boasts some pretty fin de siècle architecture, and an abundance of wine bars and shops in which to try the local tipple. *Avinguda Jaume Codorníu, Sant Sadurní d'Anoia, T 93 891 3342, www.codorniu.es*

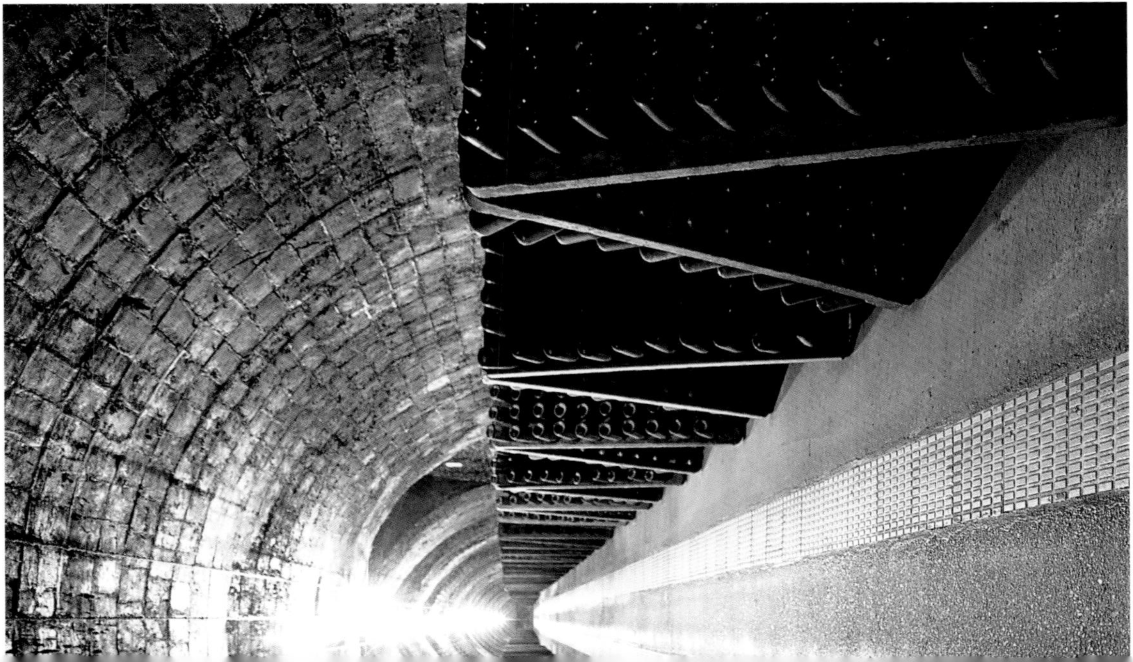

Cadaqués

Spain's easternmost coastal town sits in splendid isolation behind the Cap de Creus nature reserve, and its whitewashed charm makes it a destination of choice for discerning Catalonians. In the early 20th century, it became an artists' haunt; Picasso painted much of his early Cubist work in Cadaqués, while Salvador Dalí spent his childhood summers here. Dalí and his wife, Gala, bought a cluster of fishermen's houses in Portlligat, which is located ten minutes north of town, transforming them into a labyrinthine home (above). Now a museum (T 97 225 1015), the house offers a glimpse into the lifestyle of the sultan of surrealism. It's advisable to book a tour, as there is only capacity for eight visitors at a time.

Girona

Many visitors to Barcelona resolve to up sticks from their native land and emigrate to the city, only to discover that droves of Europeans have beaten them to it and property prices have become prohibitive. In 2008, Spain's high-speed AVE train will stop in the old Catalan town of Girona, where locals enjoy one of the highest standards of living in Spain. The commute into Barcelona Sants will be a mere 20 minutes, making property in the area (overleaf) a solid investment. Make an appointment with a local agent, such as Mandarina Houses (T 97 237 4253), and, with a list of preferred properties in hand, reserve a table at legendary restaurant Les Cols (above; T 97 226 9209) for dinner.

Begur, Girona province

NOTES

SKETCHES AND MEMOS

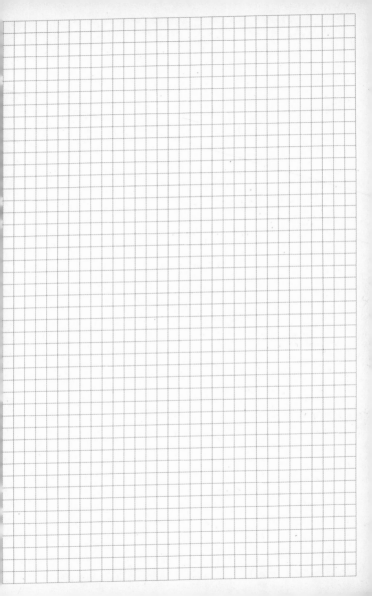

RESOURCES

CITY GUIDE DIRECTORY

A

Agua 070
  Passieg Marítim 30
  T 93 225 1272
Al Fresco 097
  Carrer Mayor 33
  Sitges
  T 93 894 0600

B

Bar Pinotxo 070
  La Boqueria 466-467
  La Rambla 91
  T 93 317 1731
Bike Rental Barcelona 088
  T 666 057 655
  www.bikerentalbarcelona.com
Bodega Codorníu 098
  Avinguda Jaume Codorníu
  Sant Sadurní d'Anoia
  T 93 891 3342
  www.codorniu.es
El Bulli 048
  Cala Montjoi
  Roses
  Girona province
  T 97 215 0457
  www.elbulli.com

C

CaixaForum 040
  Avinguda del Marquès de Comillas 6-8
  T 93 476 8600
  www.fundacio.lacaixa.es
Cal Pep 070
  Plaça de les Olles 8
  T 93 310 7961
  www.calpep.com

Can Ravell 048
  Carrer Aragó 313
  T 93 457 5114
  www.ravell.com
Casa Batlló 044
  Passeig de Gràcia 43
  T 93 216 0306
  www.casabatllo.es
Casa Calvet 048
  Carrer de Casp 48
  T 93 412 4012
  www.casacalvet.es
Casa Milà 014
  Carrer Provença 261-265
  www.lapedreraeducacio.org
Casa-Museu Salvador Dalí 100
  Portlligat
  Cadaqués
  T 97 225 1015
  www.salvador-dali.org
Castañer 080
  Carrer Mestre Nicolau 23
  T 93 414 2428
  www.castaner.com
Cata 1.81 060
  Carrer València 181
  T 93 323 6818
Cau Ferrat Museum 097
  Carrer Fonollar 8
  Sitges
  T 93 894 0364
CCCB 042
  Montalegre 5
  T 93 306 4100
  www.cccb.org
Cdlc 070
  Passeig Marítim 32
  T 93 224 0470
  www.cdlcbarcelona.com

HOTELS

ADDRESSES AND ROOM RATES

Hotel 54 038
Room rates:
double, €135
Passeig Joan de Borbó 54
T 93 225 0054

Hotel 1898 016
Room rates:
double, from €225
La Rambla 109
T 93 552 9552
www.nnhotels.com

AC Miramar 016
Room rates:
double, €195-€330;
superior, €230-€385;
suite, €395-€1,210
Plaza Carlos Ibáñez 3
T 93 281 1600
www.hotelacmiramar.com

Hotel Arts 026
Room rates:
double, €205-€550;
suite, €370-€975;
apartment, €1,300-€3,500
Carrer de la Marina 19-21
T 93 221 1000
www.ritzcarlton.com

Hotel Axel 017
Room rates:
double, from €135;
superior, from €185;
Axel Suite, from €280
Carrer Aribau 33
T 93 323 9393
www.hotelaxel.com

Casa Camper 035
Room rates:
double, €210-€245;
suite, €230-€265
Carrer Elisabets 11
T 93 342 6280
www.casacamper.com

Hotel Claris 016
Room rates:
double, €210
Pau Claris 150
T 93 487 6262
www.derbyhotels.com

Hotel Cram 016
Room rates:
double, from €185;
suite, from €370;
Privilege Suite, from €300
Carrer Aribau 54
T 93 216 7700
www.hotelcram.com

Hotel Diagonal Barcelona 022
Room rates:
double, €100-€230;
Rooms 724, 824, €100-€230;
suite, €250-€350
Avenida Diagonal 205
T 93 489 5300
www.hoteldiagonalbarcelona.com

Gran Hotel La Florida 019
Room rates:
double, €400-€900;
suite, €775-€825;
Japanese, Penthouse, Tibidabo, Tower
Terrace Suites, all €1,500
Carretera de Vallvidrera
al Tibidabo 83-93
T 93 259 3000
www.hotellaflorida.com

Hesperia Tower 031
  Room rates:
  double, €130-€190;
  suite, €250-€340;
  Presidential Suite, €960
  Mare de Déu de Bellvitge 1
  T 93 413 5000
  www.hesperia-tower.com

Mas de Torrent 096
  Room rates:
  double, from €295
  Afores de Torrent
  Torrent
  T 90 255 0321
  www.mastorrent.com

Le Méridien Ra Beach Hotel & Spa 028
  Room rates:
  deluxe, €245-€290;
  premium, €320-€350;
  grand deluxe, €380-€410;
  prestige, €460;
  duplex, €560;
  presidential, €1,300
  Avinguda Sanatori 1
  Platja de Sant Salvador
  El Vendrell
  T 97 769 4200
  www.lemeridien.com

Hotel Neri 024
  Room rates:
  double, €285-€375;
  suite, €340-€440
  Carrer Sant Sever 5
  T 93 304 0655
  www.hotelneri.com

Hotel Omm 032
  Room rates:
  double and rooms 501, 601,
  €200-€675;
  suite, €400-€520
  Carrer Rosselló 265
  T 93 454 4000
  www.hotelomm.es

Hotel Pulitzer 036
  Room rates:
  double, €100-€300;
  Rooms 306, 506, €160-€300
  Carrer de Bergara 8
  T 93 481 6767
  www.hotelpulitzer.es

Hotel Soho 039
  Room rates:
  double, €110-€310
  Gran Via 543-545
  T 93 552 9610
  www.nnhotels.es

WALLPAPER* CITY GUIDES

Editorial Director
Richard Cook

Art Director
Loran Stosskopf
Editor
Rachael Moloney
Authors
Jeroen Bergmans
Suzanne Wales
Managing Editor
Jessica Firmin

Chief Designer
Ben Blossom
Designers
Dominic Bell
Sara Martin
Ingvild Sandal

Map Illustrator
Russell Bell

Photography Editor
Emma Blau
Photography Assistant
Jasmine Labeau

Sub-Editors
Sarah Frank
Paul Sentobe

Editorial Assistant
Milly Nolan

**Wallpaper* Group
Editor-in-Chief**
Tony Chambers
Publishing Director
Gord Ray
Publisher
Neil Sumner

Contributors
Paul Barnes
Sara Henrichs
Emma Moore
Meirion Pritchard

Wallpaper* ® is a
registered trademark
of IPC Media Limited

All prices are correct at
time of going to press,
but are subject to change.

Printed in China

PHAIDON

Phaidon Press Limited
Regent's Wharf
All Saints Street
London N1 9PA

Phaidon Press Inc
180 Varick Street
New York, NY 10014

Phaidon® is a registered
trademark of Phaidon
Press Limited

www.phaidon.com

First published 2006
Second edition (revised
and updated) 2008
© 2006 and 2008
IPC Media Limited

ISBN 978 0 7148 4827 3

A CIP Catalogue record for
this book is available from
the British Library.

PHOTOGRAPHERS

Palmer Aldritch
Mercat de Santa Caterina,
pp010-011
Torre Agbar, p012
Gran Hotel La
Florida, p018
Hotel Neri, pp024-025
Hotel Omm, p032
CCCB, pp042-043
Casa Batlló, p044
Sagrada Família, p045
Sugar Club, p046
Il Giardinetto, p047
Flash Flash, p049
Torre d'Alta Mar,
pp050-051
Cinq Sentis, p053
Cata 1.81, p060
Noti, p061
Gimlet, pp066-067
Alex Al-Bader, p071
Vinçon, p084
Six Senses Spa, pp092-093

Jeroen Bergmans
Sitges, p097

Roger Casas
Hotel Axel, p017
Tapioles 53, p052
Mondo, p057
Inopia Classic Bar,
pp064-065
Dry Martini, p068
Negroni, p069
Edifici Fòrum, p077
Edifici Gas Natural, p078
Diagonal Mar Park, p079
Coquette, p081

Gregori Civera
Barcelona city view,
inside front cover
Casa Milà, pp014-015
Cuines Santa Caterina,
p041
Taller de Arquitectura,
p073

**Gala-Salvador Dalí
Foundation**
Cadaqués Dalí Museum
(images kindly given, all
rights reserved), p100

Ben Johnson
Montjuïc Communications
Tower, p013

**Pepo Segura, Fundació
Mies van der Rohe,
Barcelona**
Mies van der Rohe
Pavilion, pp074-075

Morley von Sternberg
Llogbregat Sports Centre,
pp094-095

BARCELONA

A COLOUR-CODED GUIDE TO THE CITY'S HOT 'HOODS

LA BARCELONETA
All steel and skyscrapers, this is the brash new town that the Olympics left behind

BARRI GÒTIC
Barcelona's historic heart is lorded over by the flamboyant cathedral

EL BORN
The best shopping in town; somewhere in the jumble of streets is the Museu Picasso

L'EIXAMPLE
This heartland of the *modernista* movement is the first port of call for Gaudí fans

GRÀCIA
Often ignored by tourists en route to Park Güell, but currently the city's hottest 'hood

EL POBLENOU
The centre of the city's nightlife and home to the new generation of loft-living locals

POBLE SEC
For a change of pace, head to the leafy squares and quiet streets of this charming area

EL RAVAL
Now arguably the city's cultural capital, El Raval is packed with bars and boutiques

SANT PERE
For a sedate vision of the city as it used to be, head here. But do it fast

For a full description of each neighbourhood, see the Introduction.
Featured venues are colour-coded, according to the district in which they are located.